50 Traditional Thai Recipes for Home Cooks

By: Kelly Johnson

Table of Contents

- Pad Thai
- Tom Yum Goong (Spicy Shrimp Soup)
- Green Curry (Gaeng Keow Wan)
- Red Curry (Gaeng Phed)
- Massaman Curry
- Panang Curry
- Tom Kha Gai (Chicken Coconut Soup)
- Som Tum (Green Papaya Salad)
- Larb Gai (Spicy Chicken Salad)
- Pad Kra Pao (Basil Chicken)
- Pad See Ew (Stir-Fried Flat Noodles)
- Khao Pad (Thai Fried Rice)
- Moo Ping (Grilled Pork Skewers)
- Gai Yang (Thai Grilled Chicken)
- Thai Fish Cakes (Tod Mun Pla)
- Pla Rad Prik (Crispy Fish with Chili Sauce)
- Gaeng Som (Sour Curry)
- Thai Beef Salad (Yum Nua)
- Khao Soi (Curry Noodle Soup)
- Thai Pineapple Fried Rice
- Sticky Rice with Mango (Khao Niew Mamuang)
- Thai Iced Tea (Cha Yen)
- Satay with Peanut Sauce
- Thai Spring Rolls
- Thai Vegetable Stir Fry (Pad Pak Ruam Mit)
- Spicy Glass Noodle Salad (Yum Woon Sen)
- Thai Fried Bananas (Kluai Tod)
- Thai Crab Omelet (Khai Jiao Poo)
- Thai Spicy Squid (Pla Muek Pad Kee Mao)
- Chicken Satay
- Thai Pumpkin Curry
- Thai Hot Pot (Jim Jum)
- Thai Eggplant Stir-Fry
- Thai Beef Massaman Curry
- Pad Prik King (Stir-Fried Red Curry with Green Beans)

- Thai Garlic Pepper Chicken (Gai Pad Gratiem Prik Thai)
- Pad Woon Sen (Stir-Fried Glass Noodles)
- Thai Lemongrass Chicken Soup
- Thai Shrimp Paste Chili Dip (Nam Prik Kapi)
- Thai Coconut Pancakes (Khanom Krok)
- Thai Green Mango Salad
- Thai Grilled Sticky Rice (Khao Jee)
- Thai Chicken and Rice (Khao Man Gai)
- Thai Sweet Sticky Rice with Custard
- Thai Herb Salad (Yam Pak Kood)
- Thai Pumpkin Custard (Sangkaya Fak Thong)
- Thai Chicken Wings (Peek Gai Tod)
- Thai Spicy Shrimp Salad (Pla Goong)
- Thai Grilled Eggplant Salad (Yam Makheua Yao)
- Thai Milk Tea Popsicles

Pad Thai

Ingredients

- **Noodles**:
    - 8 oz rice noodles
- **Sauce**:
    - 3 tbsp fish sauce
    - 1 tbsp tamarind paste
    - 1 tbsp sugar
    - 1 tbsp lime juice
    - 1 tsp chili powder (adjust to taste)
- **Protein**:
    - 1 cup shrimp, chicken, or tofu (cubed)
- **Vegetables**:
    - 2 cloves garlic (minced)
    - 2 green onions (sliced)
    - 1 cup bean sprouts
    - 1/2 cup carrots (julienned)
- **Toppings**:
    - Crushed peanuts
    - Lime wedges
    - Fresh cilantro

Instructions

1. **Prepare Noodles**:
   Soak the rice noodles in warm water for about 20-30 minutes until soft. Drain and set aside.
2. **Make Sauce**:
   In a small bowl, mix together fish sauce, tamarind paste, sugar, lime juice, and chili powder. Stir until the sugar dissolves.
3. **Cook Protein**:
   In a large pan or wok over medium-high heat, add a bit of oil and cook your chosen protein until fully cooked. Remove from the pan and set aside.
4. **Sauté Vegetables**:
   In the same pan, add a little more oil if necessary and sauté garlic until fragrant. Add the carrots and cook for a few minutes, then add the green onions and drained noodles.

5. **Combine**:
   Pour the sauce over the noodles and stir-fry for about 2-3 minutes until everything is well coated and heated through. Add the protein back into the pan along with the bean sprouts and toss everything together.
6. **Serve**:
   Divide the Pad Thai onto plates and top with crushed peanuts, lime wedges, and fresh cilantro. Enjoy your meal!

Tom Yum Goong (Spicy Shrimp Soup)

Ingredients

- 8 cups water or chicken broth
- 1 stalk lemongrass (cut into 2-inch pieces and smashed)
- 5-6 kaffir lime leaves (torn)
- 3-4 slices galangal (or ginger)
- 200 g shrimp (peeled and deveined)
- 200 g mushrooms (sliced)
- 2-3 Thai bird chilies (smashed, adjust to taste)
- 3 tbsp fish sauce
- 1 tbsp lime juice
- 1 tsp sugar
- Fresh cilantro (for garnish)

Instructions

1. In a pot, bring the water or chicken broth to a boil. Add lemongrass, kaffir lime leaves, and galangal.
2. Simmer for about 10 minutes to infuse the flavors.
3. Add shrimp and mushrooms, cooking until the shrimp turns pink.
4. Stir in the chilies, fish sauce, lime juice, and sugar. Adjust seasoning to taste.
5. Serve hot, garnished with fresh cilantro.

Green Curry (Gaeng Keow Wan)

Ingredients

- 1 can (400 ml) coconut milk
- 2-3 tbsp green curry paste
- 400 g chicken (sliced thinly)
- 1 cup eggplant (cubed)
- 1 cup bamboo shoots (drained)
- 1 red bell pepper (sliced)
- 1-2 tbsp fish sauce
- 1 tbsp palm sugar (or brown sugar)
- 5-6 kaffir lime leaves (torn)
- Fresh Thai basil (for garnish)

Instructions

1. In a pot, heat half of the coconut milk over medium heat until it bubbles. Add green curry paste and stir until fragrant.
2. Add the chicken and cook until no longer pink.
3. Pour in the remaining coconut milk and add eggplant, bamboo shoots, and bell pepper. Cook until vegetables are tender.
4. Stir in fish sauce, palm sugar, and kaffir lime leaves. Adjust seasoning if needed.
5. Serve hot, garnished with fresh Thai basil.

Red Curry (Gaeng Phed)

Ingredients

- 1 can (400 ml) coconut milk
- 2-3 tbsp red curry paste
- 400 g beef, chicken, or tofu (sliced thinly)
- 1 cup bell peppers (sliced)
- 1 cup zucchini (sliced)
- 1 cup Thai basil (or sweet basil)
- 1-2 tbsp fish sauce
- 1 tbsp palm sugar (or brown sugar)
- Fresh cilantro (for garnish)

Instructions

1. In a pot, heat half of the coconut milk over medium heat. Add red curry paste and stir until fragrant.
2. Add the meat or tofu and cook until browned.
3. Pour in the remaining coconut milk and add bell peppers and zucchini. Simmer until vegetables are tender.
4. Stir in fish sauce and palm sugar. Adjust to taste.
5. Serve hot, garnished with fresh cilantro.

Feel free to adjust the spice levels and ingredients according to your preferences! Enjoy your cooking!

Massaman Curry

Ingredients

- 1 can (400 ml) coconut milk
- 3-4 tbsp Massaman curry paste
- 400 g beef or chicken (cut into chunks)
- 2 medium potatoes (peeled and cubed)
- 1 onion (sliced)
- 1-2 tbsp fish sauce
- 1 tbsp tamarind paste
- 1 tbsp palm sugar (or brown sugar)
- 1 cup roasted peanuts
- Fresh cilantro (for garnish)

Instructions

1. In a pot, heat half of the coconut milk over medium heat. Add Massaman curry paste and cook until fragrant.
2. Add the beef or chicken and cook until browned.
3. Pour in the remaining coconut milk, potatoes, and onion. Simmer until the meat is tender.
4. Stir in fish sauce, tamarind paste, palm sugar, and peanuts. Cook for a few more minutes.
5. Serve hot, garnished with fresh cilantro.

Panang Curry

Ingredients

- 1 can (400 ml) coconut milk
- 2-3 tbsp Panang curry paste
- 400 g beef or chicken (sliced thinly)
- 1 cup bell peppers (sliced)
- 1-2 tbsp fish sauce
- 1 tbsp palm sugar (or brown sugar)
- 5-6 kaffir lime leaves (torn)
- Fresh Thai basil (for garnish)

Instructions

1. In a pot, heat half of the coconut milk over medium heat. Add Panang curry paste and cook until fragrant.
2. Add the meat and cook until no longer pink.
3. Pour in the remaining coconut milk and add bell peppers. Simmer until the peppers are tender.
4. Stir in fish sauce, palm sugar, and kaffir lime leaves. Adjust seasoning as needed.
5. Serve hot, garnished with fresh Thai basil.

Tom Kha Gai (Chicken Coconut Soup)

Ingredients

- 4 cups chicken broth
- 1 can (400 ml) coconut milk
- 1 stalk lemongrass (cut into 2-inch pieces and smashed)
- 5-6 kaffir lime leaves (torn)
- 3-4 slices galangal (or ginger)
- 400 g chicken (sliced thinly)
- 200 g mushrooms (sliced)
- 2-3 Thai bird chilies (smashed, adjust to taste)
- 3 tbsp fish sauce
- 1 tbsp lime juice
- Fresh cilantro (for garnish)

Instructions

1. In a pot, bring the chicken broth to a boil. Add lemongrass, kaffir lime leaves, and galangal.
2. Simmer for about 10 minutes to infuse the flavors.
3. Add the chicken and mushrooms, cooking until the chicken is cooked through.
4. Stir in the chilies, fish sauce, lime juice, and adjust seasoning to taste.
5. Serve hot, garnished with fresh cilantro.

Som Tum (Green Papaya Salad)

Ingredients

- 2 cups green papaya (shredded)
- 1 cup carrots (shredded)
- 1-2 Thai bird chilies (smashed, adjust to taste)
- 3 tbsp fish sauce
- 2 tbsp lime juice
- 1 tbsp palm sugar (or brown sugar)
- 1/4 cup peanuts (crushed)
- Cherry tomatoes (halved, optional)

Instructions

1. In a large bowl, combine shredded papaya, carrots, and cherry tomatoes.
2. In a mortar and pestle, pound the chilies, fish sauce, lime juice, and palm sugar until mixed.
3. Pour the dressing over the salad and toss well.
4. Top with crushed peanuts before serving.

Larb Gai (Spicy Chicken Salad)

Ingredients

- 400 g ground chicken
- 1/4 cup rice (toasted and ground into powder)
- 1/2 onion (finely chopped)
- 2-3 Thai bird chilies (smashed, adjust to taste)
- 3 tbsp fish sauce
- 2 tbsp lime juice
- Fresh mint leaves (for garnish)
- Lettuce leaves (for serving)

Instructions

1. In a pan, cook ground chicken until fully cooked. Remove from heat and let cool.
2. In a bowl, combine the chicken with ground rice, onion, chilies, fish sauce, and lime juice. Mix well.
3. Serve in lettuce leaves, garnished with fresh mint leaves.

Pad Kra Pao (Basil Chicken)

Ingredients

- 400 g ground chicken or pork
- 4-5 cloves garlic (minced)
- 2-3 Thai bird chilies (smashed, adjust to taste)
- 2-3 tbsp fish sauce
- 1 tbsp soy sauce
- 1 tbsp oyster sauce
- 1 tbsp sugar
- 1 cup Thai basil leaves
- Cooked jasmine rice (for serving)
- Fried egg (for serving, optional)

Instructions

1. In a pan, heat oil over medium heat and sauté garlic and chilies until fragrant.
2. Add ground chicken and cook until browned.
3. Stir in fish sauce, soy sauce, oyster sauce, and sugar. Cook for another minute.
4. Add basil leaves and stir until wilted.
5. Serve hot over jasmine rice, topped with a fried egg if desired.

Pad See Ew (Stir-Fried Flat Noodles)

Ingredients

- 8 oz wide rice noodles
- 200 g chicken, beef, or tofu (sliced)
- 2-3 cloves garlic (minced)
- 1 cup broccoli or Chinese broccoli (cut into pieces)
- 2-3 tbsp soy sauce
- 1 tbsp oyster sauce
- 1 tbsp sugar
- 1-2 eggs (beaten)
- Cooking oil (for frying)

Instructions

1. Cook the rice noodles according to package instructions and set aside.
2. In a large pan or wok, heat oil over medium-high heat. Add garlic and cook until fragrant.
3. Add the protein and cook until browned.
4. Push everything to one side and add the beaten eggs, scrambling until cooked.
5. Add the cooked noodles, broccoli, soy sauce, oyster sauce, and sugar. Stir-fry until heated through.
6. Serve hot.

Khao Pad (Thai Fried Rice)

Ingredients

- 3 cups cooked jasmine rice (preferably day-old)
- 200 g shrimp, chicken, or tofu (diced)
- 2-3 cloves garlic (minced)
- 1 cup mixed vegetables (peas, carrots, corn)
- 2-3 tbsp soy sauce
- 1 tbsp oyster sauce
- 1-2 eggs (beaten)
- Fresh cilantro (for garnish)
- Lime wedges (for serving)

Instructions

1. In a pan, heat oil over medium-high heat and sauté garlic until fragrant.
2. Add the protein and cook until fully cooked.
3. Push everything to one side and add the beaten eggs, scrambling until cooked.
4. Add the cooked rice and mixed vegetables, stir-frying well.
5. Stir in soy sauce and oyster sauce. Mix until heated through.
6. Serve hot, garnished with fresh cilantro and lime wedges.

Enjoy your cooking!

Moo Ping (Grilled Pork Skewers)

Ingredients

- 500 g pork shoulder (sliced thinly)
- 2-3 tbsp soy sauce
- 2-3 tbsp fish sauce
- 2 tbsp oyster sauce
- 2 tbsp sugar
- 3-4 cloves garlic (minced)
- 1 tsp white pepper
- Skewers (soaked in water if wooden)

Instructions

1. In a bowl, combine soy sauce, fish sauce, oyster sauce, sugar, garlic, and white pepper.
2. Add the sliced pork and marinate for at least 2 hours or overnight.
3. Preheat the grill to medium heat.
4. Thread the marinated pork onto skewers.
5. Grill for about 5-7 minutes on each side until cooked through and slightly charred.
6. Serve hot with sticky rice and a spicy dipping sauce.

Gai Yang (Thai Grilled Chicken)

Ingredients

- 1 whole chicken (about 1 kg, spatchcocked)
- 3-4 tbsp soy sauce
- 2-3 tbsp fish sauce
- 1 tbsp oyster sauce
- 2 tbsp sugar
- 4-5 cloves garlic (minced)
- 1-2 tbsp white pepper
- Fresh cilantro (for garnish)

Instructions

1. In a bowl, mix soy sauce, fish sauce, oyster sauce, sugar, garlic, and white pepper.
2. Marinate the spatchcocked chicken in the mixture for at least 2 hours or overnight.
3. Preheat the grill to medium heat.
4. Grill the chicken skin-side down for about 30 minutes, then flip and grill for another 20 minutes or until fully cooked.
5. Let rest for a few minutes, then serve garnished with fresh cilantro.

Thai Fish Cakes (Tod Mun Pla)

Ingredients

- 400 g white fish fillets (such as cod, minced)
- 1/4 cup green beans (finely chopped)
- 2-3 tbsp red curry paste
- 1-2 eggs (beaten)
- 1-2 tbsp fish sauce
- 1 tbsp lime juice
- Fresh cilantro (for garnish)
- Vegetable oil (for frying)

Instructions

1. In a bowl, combine minced fish, green beans, red curry paste, eggs, fish sauce, and lime juice. Mix until well combined.
2. Shape the mixture into small patties.
3. Heat oil in a frying pan over medium heat. Fry the patties until golden brown on both sides, about 3-4 minutes per side.
4. Drain on paper towels and serve hot, garnished with fresh cilantro and sweet chili sauce.

Pla Rad Prik (Crispy Fish with Chili Sauce)

Ingredients

- 1 whole fish (about 500 g, cleaned and scaled)
- 1 cup all-purpose flour
- Oil (for frying)
- 2-3 tbsp chili paste or sauce
- 1-2 tbsp fish sauce
- 1-2 tbsp lime juice
- 1-2 tsp sugar
- Fresh cilantro (for garnish)

Instructions

1. Heat oil in a deep pan for frying.
2. Dust the fish with flour, shaking off excess. Fry in hot oil until crispy and golden, about 5-7 minutes per side. Drain on paper towels.
3. In a small saucepan, mix chili paste, fish sauce, lime juice, and sugar over low heat until combined.
4. Pour the chili sauce over the fried fish before serving.
5. Garnish with fresh cilantro.

Gaeng Som (Sour Curry)

Ingredients

- 1 can (400 ml) coconut milk
- 2-3 tbsp sour curry paste (or adjust to taste)
- 400 g fish fillets or shrimp
- 1 cup assorted vegetables (such as green beans and bamboo shoots)
- 2-3 tbsp fish sauce
- 1-2 tbsp tamarind paste
- 1-2 tbsp sugar
- Fresh Thai basil (for garnish)

Instructions

1. In a pot, heat coconut milk over medium heat. Add sour curry paste and cook until fragrant.
2. Add the fish or shrimp and cook until they are just cooked through.
3. Stir in vegetables, fish sauce, tamarind paste, and sugar. Simmer for a few minutes until vegetables are tender.
4. Serve hot, garnished with fresh Thai basil.

Thai Beef Salad (Yum Nua)

Ingredients

- 400 g beef (grilled and thinly sliced)
- 1/2 cucumber (sliced)
- 1 cup cherry tomatoes (halved)
- 1/2 onion (sliced)
- 2-3 tbsp fish sauce
- 1-2 tbsp lime juice
- 1-2 tbsp sugar
- Fresh cilantro (for garnish)
- Lettuce leaves (for serving)

Instructions

1. In a bowl, combine fish sauce, lime juice, and sugar to make the dressing.
2. In a large bowl, combine sliced beef, cucumber, cherry tomatoes, and onion. Pour the dressing over and toss well.
3. Serve on a bed of lettuce leaves, garnished with fresh cilantro.

Khao Soi (Curry Noodle Soup)

Ingredients

- 200 g egg noodles
- 1 can (400 ml) coconut milk
- 2-3 tbsp yellow curry paste
- 400 g chicken (cut into pieces)
- 2-3 cups chicken broth
- 1-2 tbsp fish sauce
- 1 tbsp sugar
- Fresh lime wedges (for serving)
- Sliced shallots, pickled mustard greens, and fresh cilantro (for garnish)

Instructions

1. Cook egg noodles according to package instructions and set aside.
2. In a pot, heat coconut milk over medium heat. Add yellow curry paste and cook until fragrant.
3. Add chicken pieces and cook until no longer pink. Pour in chicken broth and bring to a boil. Simmer until chicken is cooked through.
4. Stir in fish sauce and sugar. Adjust seasoning if needed.
5. Serve hot over egg noodles, garnished with lime wedges, sliced shallots, pickled mustard greens, and fresh cilantro.

Thai Pineapple Fried Rice

Ingredients

- 3 cups cooked jasmine rice (preferably day-old)
- 1 cup pineapple (cubed)
- 200 g shrimp, chicken, or tofu (diced)
- 2-3 cloves garlic (minced)
- 1/2 cup peas and carrots (mixed)
- 2-3 tbsp soy sauce
- 1-2 tbsp curry powder
- 2-3 green onions (sliced)
- Fresh cilantro (for garnish)

Instructions

1. In a large pan or wok, heat oil over medium-high heat. Sauté garlic until fragrant.
2. Add the shrimp, chicken, or tofu and cook until fully cooked.
3. Stir in peas, carrots, pineapple, cooked rice, soy sauce, and curry powder. Mix well and stir-fry for a few minutes.
4. Add sliced green onions and stir until heated through.
5. Serve hot, garnished with fresh cilantro.

Sticky Rice with Mango (Khao Niew Mamuang)

Ingredients

- 1 cup glutinous (sticky) rice
- 1 1/2 cups coconut milk
- 1/2 cup sugar
- 1/4 tsp salt
- 2 ripe mangoes (sliced)
- Sesame seeds or mung beans (for garnish)

Instructions

1. Rinse the sticky rice until the water runs clear. Soak in water for at least 4 hours or overnight.
2. Drain the rice and steam it in a bamboo steamer lined with cheesecloth for about 20-30 minutes until tender.
3. In a saucepan, heat coconut milk with sugar and salt until dissolved. Reserve 1/4 cup for drizzling later.
4. Once the rice is cooked, mix it with the remaining coconut milk and let it sit for 10-15 minutes.
5. Serve the sticky rice with sliced mangoes and drizzle with reserved coconut milk. Garnish with sesame seeds or mung beans.

Thai Iced Tea (Cha Yen)

Ingredients

- 4 cups water
- 4-5 tbsp Thai tea leaves
- 1/2 cup sugar
- 1 cup evaporated milk or coconut milk
- Ice cubes

Instructions

1. Boil water in a pot and add Thai tea leaves. Let it steep for 5-10 minutes.
2. Strain the tea to remove the leaves and stir in sugar while the tea is still hot.
3. Allow the tea to cool, then refrigerate until chilled.
4. To serve, fill a glass with ice cubes, pour in the tea, and top with evaporated milk or coconut milk. Stir before drinking.

Satay with Peanut Sauce

Ingredients

- 500 g chicken or pork (cut into thin strips)
- 2-3 tbsp soy sauce
- 2-3 tbsp curry powder
- 1-2 tbsp sugar
- 2-3 cloves garlic (minced)
- Skewers (soaked in water if wooden)

Peanut Sauce Ingredients

- 1 cup creamy peanut butter
- 1/2 cup coconut milk
- 2-3 tbsp sugar
- 2-3 tbsp soy sauce
- 1-2 tbsp lime juice
- 1-2 tbsp chili sauce (optional)

Instructions

1. In a bowl, mix soy sauce, curry powder, sugar, and garlic. Marinate the meat for at least 1 hour.
2. Thread the marinated meat onto skewers.
3. Preheat the grill or pan over medium heat. Grill the skewers for about 5-7 minutes on each side until cooked through.
4. For the peanut sauce, combine peanut butter, coconut milk, sugar, soy sauce, lime juice, and chili sauce in a saucepan. Heat over low until smooth.
5. Serve the satay hot with the peanut sauce for dipping.

Thai Spring Rolls

Ingredients

- 10-12 rice paper wrappers
- 1 cup cooked shrimp or chicken (sliced)
- 1 cup lettuce (shredded)
- 1/2 cup carrots (julienned)
- 1/2 cup cucumbers (julienned)
- Fresh herbs (mint, cilantro)
- Dipping sauce (sweet chili sauce or hoisin sauce)

Instructions

1. Soak each rice paper wrapper in warm water until soft (about 10-15 seconds). Lay on a clean surface.
2. Place a small amount of shrimp, lettuce, carrots, cucumbers, and herbs in the center of the wrapper.
3. Fold the sides over the filling, then roll tightly from the bottom up.
4. Repeat with the remaining wrappers and fillings.
5. Serve with your choice of dipping sauce.

Thai Vegetable Stir Fry (Pad Pak Ruam Mit)

Ingredients

- 2 cups mixed vegetables (bell peppers, broccoli, carrots, snap peas)
- 2-3 cloves garlic (minced)
- 2-3 tbsp soy sauce
- 1-2 tbsp oyster sauce
- 1-2 tbsp vegetable oil

Instructions

1. Heat oil in a wok or large pan over medium-high heat. Add garlic and sauté until fragrant.
2. Add the mixed vegetables and stir-fry for 3-4 minutes until tender-crisp.
3. Stir in soy sauce and oyster sauce, mixing well to coat the vegetables.
4. Cook for an additional 1-2 minutes, then serve hot.

Spicy Glass Noodle Salad (Yum Woon Sen)

Ingredients

- 100 g glass noodles (mung bean noodles)
- 200 g shrimp or minced pork
- 1 cup mixed vegetables (carrots, bell peppers, onions)
- 2-3 tbsp fish sauce
- 1-2 tbsp lime juice
- 1-2 tbsp sugar
- Fresh herbs (mint, cilantro)
- Chili flakes (to taste)

Instructions

1. Soak glass noodles in hot water for about 10 minutes until softened, then drain.
2. In a pot, boil water and cook the shrimp or minced pork until fully cooked. Drain and let cool.
3. In a large bowl, combine glass noodles, shrimp or pork, mixed vegetables, fish sauce, lime juice, sugar, and herbs. Toss well.
4. Adjust seasoning with more fish sauce, lime juice, or chili flakes to taste.
5. Serve chilled or at room temperature.

Thai Fried Bananas (Kluai Tod)

Ingredients

- 4 ripe bananas (preferably Thai bananas)
- 1 cup all-purpose flour
- 1/2 cup rice flour
- 1-2 tbsp sugar
- 1/2 tsp salt
- 1 cup coconut milk
- Oil (for frying)

Instructions

1. In a bowl, mix all-purpose flour, rice flour, sugar, and salt. Gradually add coconut milk to form a smooth batter.
2. Heat oil in a frying pan over medium heat.
3. Peel and slice the bananas into halves or quarters. Dip each piece in the batter.
4. Fry the banana pieces until golden brown on all sides, about 2-3 minutes per side. Drain on paper towels.
5. Serve warm, optionally dusted with powdered sugar.

Thai Crab Omelet (Khai Jiao Poo)

Ingredients

- 4 eggs
- 200 g crab meat
- 2-3 tbsp fish sauce
- 1-2 green onions (sliced)
- Vegetable oil (for frying)
- Fresh cilantro (for garnish)

Instructions

1. In a bowl, beat the eggs and mix in crab meat, fish sauce, and green onions.
2. Heat oil in a pan over medium heat. Pour in the egg mixture and cook until the edges start to set.
3. Flip the omelet carefully and cook until fully set and golden brown on both sides.
4. Slide onto a plate and garnish with fresh cilantro before serving.

Enjoy your culinary adventures!

Thai Spicy Squid (Pla Muek Pad Kee Mao)

Ingredients

- 500 g squid (cleaned and sliced)
- 2-3 tbsp vegetable oil
- 3-4 cloves garlic (minced)
- 2-3 Thai bird's eye chilies (sliced)
- 1 cup bell peppers (sliced)
- 1 cup green beans (trimmed)
- 2-3 tbsp soy sauce
- 1-2 tbsp oyster sauce
- 1-2 tbsp fish sauce
- Fresh basil leaves (for garnish)

Instructions

1. Heat oil in a wok over medium-high heat. Add garlic and chilies, stirring until fragrant.
2. Add squid and stir-fry for 2-3 minutes until cooked.
3. Add bell peppers and green beans, cooking for an additional 2-3 minutes.
4. Stir in soy sauce, oyster sauce, and fish sauce, mixing well.
5. Serve hot, garnished with fresh basil leaves.

Chicken Satay

Ingredients

- 500 g chicken breast (cut into thin strips)
- 2-3 tbsp soy sauce
- 2-3 tbsp curry powder
- 1-2 tbsp sugar
- 2-3 cloves garlic (minced)
- Skewers (soaked in water if wooden)

Peanut Sauce Ingredients

- 1 cup creamy peanut butter
- 1/2 cup coconut milk
- 2-3 tbsp sugar
- 2-3 tbsp soy sauce
- 1-2 tbsp lime juice
- 1-2 tbsp chili sauce (optional)

Instructions

1. In a bowl, combine soy sauce, curry powder, sugar, and garlic. Marinate chicken strips for at least 1 hour.
2. Thread marinated chicken onto skewers.
3. Grill on medium heat for about 5-7 minutes on each side until cooked.
4. For peanut sauce, mix peanut butter, coconut milk, sugar, soy sauce, lime juice, and chili sauce in a saucepan over low heat until smooth.
5. Serve skewers with peanut sauce for dipping.

Thai Pumpkin Curry

Ingredients

- 400 g pumpkin (peeled and cubed)
- 1 can (400 ml) coconut milk
- 2-3 tbsp red curry paste
- 1-2 tbsp fish sauce
- 1 tbsp sugar
- 1 cup Thai basil leaves
- Optional: protein of choice (chicken, shrimp, or tofu)

Instructions

1. In a pot, combine coconut milk and red curry paste over medium heat, stirring until well mixed.
2. Add pumpkin and any protein, cooking until the pumpkin is tender (about 10-15 minutes).
3. Stir in fish sauce and sugar, adjusting to taste.
4. Remove from heat and fold in Thai basil leaves before serving.

Thai Hot Pot (Jim Jum)

Ingredients

- 500 g assorted meat (beef, chicken, pork, or seafood)
- 1 liter chicken or beef broth
- 1-2 cups vegetables (mushrooms, bok choy, spinach)
- 1-2 cups noodles (rice or egg noodles)
- 2-3 tbsp fish sauce
- 2-3 tbsp lime juice
- Fresh herbs (cilantro, mint) for garnish

Instructions

1. Bring broth to a simmer in a pot or hot pot.
2. Arrange meat, vegetables, and noodles on a platter.
3. Diners can cook their choice of meat and vegetables in the simmering broth.
4. Serve hot with a mixture of fish sauce and lime juice for dipping and garnish with fresh herbs.

Thai Eggplant Stir-Fry

Ingredients

- 300 g Thai eggplants (sliced)
- 2-3 tbsp vegetable oil
- 3-4 cloves garlic (minced)
- 1-2 tbsp soy sauce
- 1-2 tbsp oyster sauce
- 1-2 tbsp fish sauce
- Fresh basil leaves (for garnish)

Instructions

1. Heat oil in a wok over medium heat. Add garlic and sauté until fragrant.
2. Add sliced eggplants and stir-fry for 5-7 minutes until softened.
3. Stir in soy sauce, oyster sauce, and fish sauce, cooking for an additional 2-3 minutes.
4. Serve hot, garnished with fresh basil leaves.

Thai Beef Massaman Curry

Ingredients

- 500 g beef (cut into cubes)
- 1 can (400 ml) coconut milk
- 3-4 tbsp Massaman curry paste
- 2-3 potatoes (peeled and cubed)
- 1-2 tbsp fish sauce
- 1-2 tbsp sugar
- 1/2 cup roasted peanuts
- Fresh cilantro (for garnish)

Instructions

1. In a pot, heat a bit of oil and sauté the Massaman curry paste until fragrant.
2. Add beef and cook until browned, then pour in coconut milk.
3. Stir in potatoes, fish sauce, and sugar, simmering until the beef and potatoes are tender (about 30-40 minutes).
4. Add roasted peanuts just before serving and garnish with fresh cilantro.

Pad Prik King (Stir-Fried Red Curry with Green Beans)

Ingredients

- 300 g green beans (trimmed)
- 2-3 tbsp vegetable oil
- 3-4 tbsp red curry paste
- 2-3 tbsp fish sauce
- 1-2 tbsp sugar
- Optional: protein of choice (chicken, beef, or tofu)

Instructions

1. Heat oil in a wok over medium-high heat. Add red curry paste and sauté until fragrant.
2. Add green beans and any protein, stir-frying for about 5-7 minutes until cooked through.
3. Stir in fish sauce and sugar, mixing well to combine.
4. Serve hot.

Thai Garlic Pepper Chicken (Gai Pad Gratiem Prik Thai)

Ingredients

- 500 g chicken (cut into bite-sized pieces)
- 4-5 cloves garlic (minced)
- 1-2 tbsp black pepper
- 2-3 tbsp soy sauce
- 1-2 tbsp oyster sauce
- 1-2 tbsp vegetable oil
- Fresh cilantro (for garnish)

Instructions

1. Heat oil in a pan over medium heat. Add garlic and sauté until golden.
2. Add chicken and cook until browned and cooked through.
3. Stir in black pepper, soy sauce, and oyster sauce, mixing well.
4. Garnish with fresh cilantro before serving.

Pad Woon Sen (Stir-Fried Glass Noodles)

Ingredients

- 200 g glass noodles (soaked in warm water)
- 200 g mixed vegetables (carrots, bell peppers, and cabbage)
- 2-3 tbsp vegetable oil
- 2-3 cloves garlic (minced)
- 2-3 eggs (beaten)
- 3-4 tbsp soy sauce
- 1-2 tbsp oyster sauce
- 1-2 tbsp fish sauce
- Green onions (for garnish)

Instructions

1. Heat oil in a wok over medium heat. Add garlic and sauté until fragrant.
2. Add mixed vegetables and stir-fry for 2-3 minutes until tender.
3. Push vegetables to the side, add beaten eggs, and scramble until cooked.
4. Drain the glass noodles and add to the wok. Stir in soy sauce, oyster sauce, and fish sauce, mixing well.
5. Serve hot, garnished with chopped green onions.

Thai Lemongrass Chicken Soup

Ingredients

- 400 g chicken breast (sliced)
- 4 cups chicken broth
- 2-3 stalks lemongrass (bruised and chopped)
- 3-4 kaffir lime leaves (torn)
- 2-3 Thai bird's eye chilies (sliced)
- 200 g mushrooms (sliced)
- 2-3 tbsp fish sauce
- 1-2 tbsp lime juice
- Fresh cilantro (for garnish)

Instructions

1. In a pot, bring chicken broth to a boil. Add lemongrass, kaffir lime leaves, and chilies.
2. Add chicken and mushrooms, simmering until chicken is cooked through.
3. Stir in fish sauce and lime juice, adjusting to taste.
4. Serve hot, garnished with fresh cilantro.

Thai Shrimp Paste Chili Dip (Nam Prik Kapi)

Ingredients

- 2-3 tbsp shrimp paste
- 2-3 Thai bird's eye chilies (sliced)
- 2-3 cloves garlic (minced)
- 1-2 tbsp lime juice
- 1-2 tbsp sugar
- Fresh vegetables (cucumber, carrot, and green beans) for serving

Instructions

1. In a bowl, mix shrimp paste, chilies, garlic, lime juice, and sugar until well combined.
2. Adjust seasoning to taste.
3. Serve with fresh vegetables for dipping.

Thai Coconut Pancakes (Khanom Krok)

Ingredients

- 1 cup rice flour
- 1 cup coconut milk
- 1/2 cup sugar
- 1/2 tsp salt
- Optional: green onions or corn for filling

Instructions

1. In a bowl, mix rice flour, coconut milk, sugar, and salt until smooth.
2. Heat a mini pancake pan or muffin tin over medium heat. Pour a spoonful of the batter into each cup.
3. Cook until the edges are set, then add optional filling and cover with more batter.
4. Cook until the pancakes are golden and cooked through. Serve warm.

Thai Green Mango Salad

Ingredients

- 2 green mangoes (julienned)
- 1-2 carrots (julienned)
- 1/2 cup peanuts (crushed)
- 2-3 tbsp fish sauce
- 1-2 tbsp lime juice
- 1-2 tbsp sugar
- 1-2 Thai bird's eye chilies (sliced)
- Fresh cilantro (for garnish)

Instructions

1. In a large bowl, combine green mango, carrots, and peanuts.
2. In a separate bowl, mix fish sauce, lime juice, sugar, and chilies until well combined.
3. Pour the dressing over the salad and toss to combine.
4. Serve chilled, garnished with fresh cilantro.

Thai Grilled Sticky Rice (Khao Jee)

Ingredients

- 2 cups sticky rice (soaked for 4 hours)
- 1-2 tbsp coconut milk
- Banana leaves (for wrapping)

Instructions

1. Drain the soaked sticky rice and mix with coconut milk.
2. Shape the rice into patties and wrap in banana leaves.
3. Grill on medium heat for about 10-15 minutes until cooked through.
4. Serve warm.

Thai Chicken and Rice (Khao Man Gai)

Ingredients

- 500 g chicken (whole or cut into pieces)
- 4 cups chicken broth
- 2 cups jasmine rice
- 3-4 cloves garlic (minced)
- 2-3 tbsp soy sauce
- 1-2 tbsp fish sauce
- Cucumber and cilantro (for garnish)

Instructions

1. In a pot, bring chicken broth to a boil and add chicken, simmering until cooked.
2. Remove chicken and set aside. Strain the broth and use it to cook the jasmine rice.
3. In a separate pan, sauté garlic until fragrant, then add the cooked rice and mix well.
4. Serve chicken on a bed of rice, drizzled with soy sauce and fish sauce, garnished with cucumber and cilantro.

Thai Sweet Sticky Rice with Custard

Ingredients

- 1 cup sticky rice (soaked for 4 hours)
- 1 cup coconut milk
- 1/2 cup sugar
- 1/2 tsp salt
- 3 eggs
- 1/2 cup rice flour

Instructions

1. Drain the sticky rice and steam it until cooked through.
2. In a bowl, mix coconut milk, sugar, salt, eggs, and rice flour until smooth.
3. Pour half of the coconut mixture over the cooked sticky rice and mix well.
4. Pour the remaining mixture on top and steam for another 20-30 minutes until set. Serve warm or chilled.

Thai Herb Salad (Yam Pak Kood)

Ingredients

- 200 g mixed herbs (mint, cilantro, basil)
- 1 cucumber (sliced)
- 1-2 carrots (shredded)
- 2-3 tbsp fish sauce
- 1-2 tbsp lime juice
- 1-2 tbsp sugar
- Thai bird's eye chilies (sliced, optional)

Instructions

1. In a large bowl, combine mixed herbs, cucumber, and carrots.
2. In a separate bowl, whisk together fish sauce, lime juice, sugar, and chilies.
3. Pour the dressing over the salad and toss to combine.
4. Serve chilled.

Enjoy making these delicious Thai dishes!

Thai Pumpkin Custard (Sangkaya Fak Thong)

Ingredients

- 1 medium pumpkin (halved and seeds removed)
- 1 cup coconut milk
- 1/2 cup sugar
- 1/2 tsp salt
- 3 large eggs
- 1/2 cup rice flour (optional, for thicker custard)

Instructions

1. Steam the pumpkin halves until tender. Scoop out the flesh and mash it in a bowl.
2. In a separate bowl, whisk together coconut milk, sugar, salt, and eggs until smooth.
3. Stir in the mashed pumpkin and rice flour (if using) until well combined.
4. Pour the mixture back into the pumpkin halves or a greased baking dish.
5. Steam for about 30-40 minutes until the custard is set. Allow to cool before slicing and serving.

Thai Chicken Wings (Peek Gai Tod)

Ingredients

- 1 kg chicken wings
- 2-3 tbsp soy sauce
- 2-3 tbsp fish sauce
- 1-2 tbsp garlic (minced)
- 1-2 tbsp sugar
- 1-2 tsp black pepper
- Oil for frying

Instructions

1. In a bowl, combine soy sauce, fish sauce, garlic, sugar, and black pepper. Add chicken wings and marinate for at least 1 hour.
2. Heat oil in a deep pan over medium heat. Fry the wings in batches until golden brown and cooked through.
3. Drain on paper towels and serve hot with a dipping sauce.

Thai Spicy Shrimp Salad (Pla Goong)

Ingredients

- 400 g cooked shrimp (peeled and deveined)
- 1-2 stalks lemongrass (finely sliced)
- 2-3 kaffir lime leaves (torn)
- 2-3 Thai bird's eye chilies (sliced)
- 2-3 tbsp fish sauce
- 2-3 tbsp lime juice
- Fresh herbs (mint and cilantro) for garnish

Instructions

1. In a bowl, combine shrimp, lemongrass, kaffir lime leaves, and chilies.
2. In a separate bowl, mix fish sauce and lime juice. Pour over the shrimp mixture and toss to combine.
3. Serve chilled, garnished with fresh herbs.

Thai Grilled Eggplant Salad (Yam Makheua Yao)

Ingredients

- 2-3 long eggplants (grilled until charred and tender)
- 2-3 Thai bird's eye chilies (sliced)
- 2-3 tbsp fish sauce
- 1-2 tbsp lime juice
- 1-2 cloves garlic (minced)
- Fresh herbs (mint and cilantro) for garnish

Instructions

1. Peel the grilled eggplants and chop them into bite-sized pieces.
2. In a bowl, combine eggplants, chilies, fish sauce, lime juice, and garlic. Mix well.
3. Serve garnished with fresh herbs.

Thai Milk Tea Popsicles

Ingredients

- 2 cups brewed Thai tea (cooled)
- 1 cup coconut milk
- 1/2 cup sugar (adjust to taste)
- Pinch of salt

Instructions

1. In a bowl, mix brewed Thai tea, coconut milk, sugar, and salt until the sugar is dissolved.
2. Pour the mixture into popsicle molds and insert sticks.
3. Freeze for at least 4-6 hours or until solid. Unmold and serve chilled.

www.ingramcontent.com/pod-product-compliance
Lightning Source LLC
LaVergne TN
LVHW081329060526
838201LV00055B/2540